This book belongs to:

_____

_____

Alphabet

ALAIN GRÉE

Alphabet

Button
BOOKS

First published 2012 by Button Books, an imprint of Guild of Master
Craftsman Publications Ltd, Castle Place, 166 High Street, Lewes,
East Sussex BN7 1XU.

Text © GMC Publications Ltd, 2012 Copyright in the Work ©
GMC Publications Ltd, 2012 Illustrations © 2012 A.G. & RicoBel.
ISBN 978 1 90898 501 9

A catalogue record for this book is available from the British Library.
Publisher: Jonathan Bailey; Production Manager: Jim Bulley; Managing
Editor: Gerrie Purcell; Senior Project Editor: Dominique Page; Managing
Art Editor: Gilda Pacitti; Colour origination by GMC Reprographics;
Printed and bound in China by Leo Paper Products.

alligator

ambulance

A a

Andy and Annie are picking apples from the apple tree.

apple

bee

bus

B b

Bill's bus is extra busy today.

8

butterfly

bird

brown bear

9

caravan

car

Cc

cow

cabbage

10

carrots

cowboy

cake

camera

crab

11

dancing

dogs

D d

doll

ducks

E e

envelope

eggs

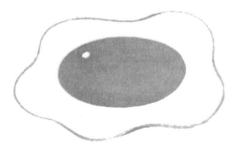

elephant

electricity

engine

fish

feather

F f

football

fire engine

fire fighters

17

garden

greenhouse

goat

G g

girl

goose

H h

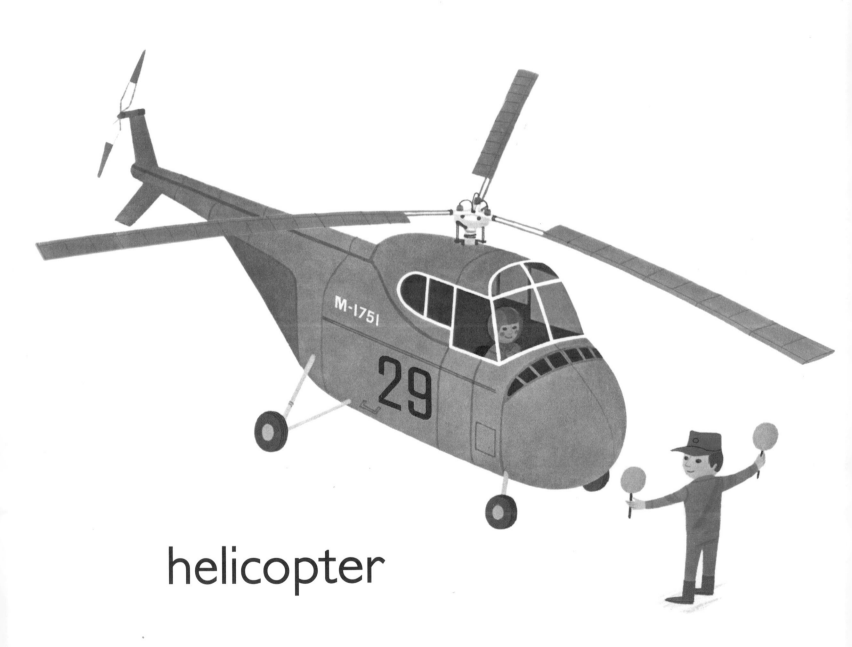

helicopter

house

hedgehog

21

Ian the Inuit boy has received an invitation from India.

igloo

I i

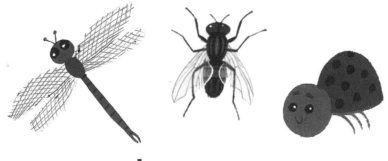

insects

J j

jumper

jet plane

juice

jam

24

kitten

Kk

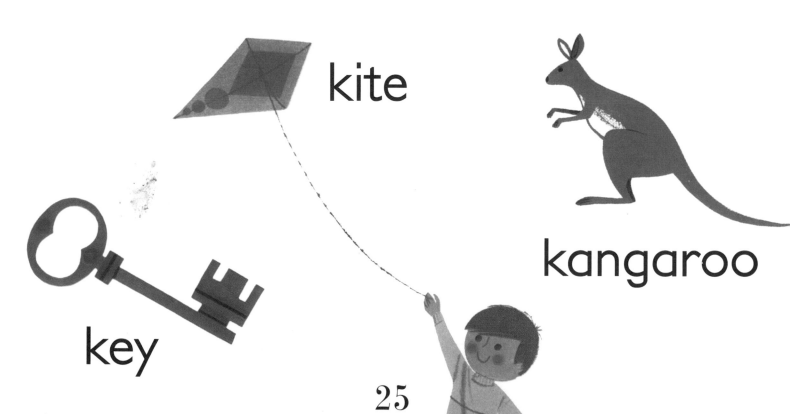

kite

key

kangaroo

leaves

Ll

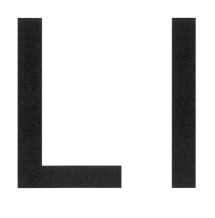

lion

lemon

lighthouse

music

Mm

milk

mice

mittens

motorbike

N n

newspaper

night

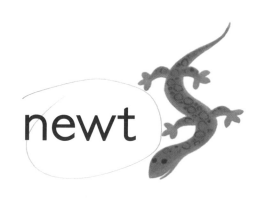

newt

nest

orchard

Oo

32

oranges

Olivia has been picking oranges in the orchard.

33

P p

parachute

puppet

parrot

pear

34

quiz

Q q

rabbit

Ronnie the rabbit really loves reading.

Rr

roundabout

rose

robin

Ss

sleigh

Simon and Sophie are going
skiing on the snowy slopes.

snowman

snow

skis

scarf

sledges

39

tennis

taxi

T t

tractor

tomato

train set

umbrella

U u

Viking

V v

van

violin

43

windmill

The windmill owner waves to his friend, William.

wheelbarrow

woof!

worm

Ww

X x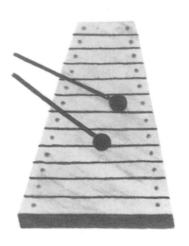

xylophone

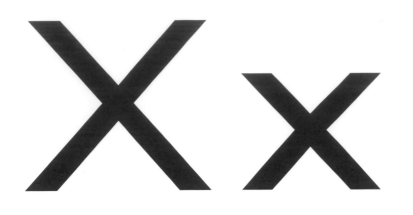

yellow

Y y

yacht

zoo

Z z

zebra

ALAIN GRÉE

For more on Button Books, contact:

GMC Publications Ltd
Castle Place, 166 High Street, Lewes, East Sussex, BN7 1XU
United Kingdom
Tel +44 (0)1273 488005
www.gmcbooks.com